THE
MESSAGE
of a
MASTER

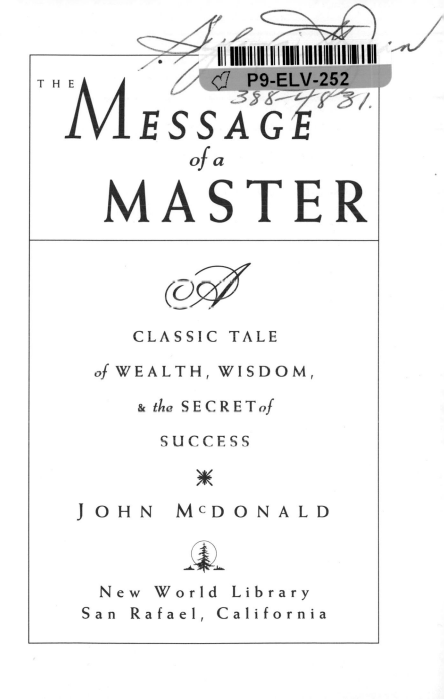

CLASSIC TALE
of WEALTH, WISDOM,
& the SECRET of
SUCCESS

JOHN McDONALD

New World Library
San Rafael, California

Original version © 1929 by A.D. McDonald
This version © 1993 New World Library

Published by New World Library
58 Paul Drive, San Rafael, CA 94903

Editing: Katherine Dieter and Marc Allen
Cover design: Kathy Warinner
Typesetting: TBH Typecast, Inc.

Library of Congress Cataloging-in-Publication Data

McDonald, John.
      Message of a master : a classic tale of wealth, wisdom, and the secret of success. / by John McDonald.
      p. cm.
ISBN 0-931432-95-2 (acid-free paper)
      1. Success.   2. McDonald, John.   I. Title.
BJ1611.M475 1993
158 — dc20   91-38486
                                                            CIP

First printing, April 1993
Printed in the U.S.A. on acid-free paper
10   9   8   7   6   5   4   3   2   1

Dedicated to my brother,
whose arrival brought a turning point in my life
and comfort and happiness into the lives
of my family.

— John McDonald

Contents

Publisher's Preface

*F*INDING A BOOK such as *The Message of a Master* is one of the greatest joys of my work and my life.

Like many great discoveries, it came from an unlikely source. A truck driver who delivered a load of books to us thought we might be interested in one of his favorite books, one that had been written years ago and was now out of print: *The Message of a Master*. He gave us his only copy, a small, well-worn hardcover edition.

We could find very little about the origin of this miraculous little piece of work. It was first published in 1929 by a company called California Press, which is no longer in business. And we could find no information about its author. All we know is that he must have been an exceptional person in order to write a book of such simplicity, usefulness, and power.

This is a book to study in depth. As the author writes in his brief message to the reader, "Should any ideas occur to you concerning your work or ambitions, lay the book aside for a few moments and meditate on them. Many profitable ideas have come to readers in this way."

I have studied this book in depth, and will continue to do so. It is a powerful tool for transformation.

— Marc Allen
New World Library

To the Reader

T HE FOLLOWING PAGES are the result of a series of notes collected and set down in the form of a story and a system of practice. The order as originally received has been carefully adhered to so that its value to the reader isn't diminished.

It sets forth no creed or dogma, but teaches in a clear, understandable, simple way, step by step, a practical, workable procedure, based on Universal Law, for the mastery of our conditions in life.

There is surely an unexplainable "something" within its pages that carries a wonderful power of helpfulness, something that saturates the reader with a dynamic conviction and realization of what it teaches.

This book is not to be hurriedly or superficially read. It must be studied to receive the priceless wisdom it contains. It is strongly urged that, after reading it once or twice, you give it slow, deep, deliberate study.

Read it as though it were a message directed to no one but yourself. Try to reason out each proposition to your satisfaction, and to get the spirit behind the words. Then apply its teachings to fit your own nature and understanding. Should any ideas occur to you concerning your work or ambitions, lay the book aside for a few moments and meditate on them. Many profitable ideas have come to readers in this way.

I am sure that there are many who are just as skeptical concerning things bordering on the extraordinary as I have been practically all my life; I offer the following story and system of practice to readers for what it's worth. Read it with a mind that is open to its possibilities, then take it or leave it as you see fit.

PART ONE
The Search

* *1* *

I am master of my own destiny, and I can make my life anything that I wish it to be.

I T WAS FRIDAY afternoon, and I had returned from a late lunch. The employees had left for the day and I was alone in the office. Business had been dropping off steadily for some time, and I was concerned. I had also put far too great a percentage of my limited cash reserves into a risky investment that had been a failure. All in all, things didn't look good; in fact, I was facing some of the most serious problems of my business career.

As I was sitting in deep thought trying to resolve some of my problems, the phone rang. I heard the familiar voice of an old friend, and it startled me. Less than a month earlier, he had left for Europe on the urgent advice of his physician. He had been told to take an ocean voyage, in the hope that a change would improve his health. He had been deeply worried over conditions that, strangely, were very similar to what I was currently experiencing. He became so depressed that he had a serious breakdown.

My last impression of him as we parted was particularly sad: He was miserable, beaten and defeated, and I wondered if I would ever see him again. But here he was back again, and some great change had taken place in him. He spoke with such striking power and feeling that I told him a miracle must have happened. He assured me I had guessed about right.

"I know you're surprised I'm back so soon; you probably never expected to see me again! But I'm back, and I'm the luckiest man in the world. I learned something that I never knew existed. Nothing is impossible for me any more. I can do anything. I am master of my own destiny, and I can make my life anything that I wish it to be. Now don't think I'm crazy — wait until you hear my story."

I laughed, but it was a laugh of surprise and concern. I asked if he had discovered some new kind of religion.

"Oh no, it concerns no religion of any kind. But I met a man, a man who is truly a Master, a wonderful man who has developed his powers so that he can do anything. He taught me an invaluable secret.

"You know that I lost my health and my money. Well, I have regained my health, and I will have new wealth in no time."

I was anxious to hear his story, of course, and we arranged to meet at our club that evening.

"Meet me there tonight, and I will unfold a series of the most remarkable things that could happen to anyone," he said.

I sat for a few minutes like someone in a dream, completely absorbed in the possibilities of what I might be told. I had the feeling that I had suddenly grown too big for my office — that I had outgrown the little place and had to get outside and expand in the fresh air. I was feverish with excitement. I felt there was something wonderful for me in his story, and I couldn't wait to hear it. I spent the rest of the day restlessly pacing the streets, and was greatly relieved when the hour to go to the club finally arrived.

When I entered the club, I was told that my friend had called some time before to say that something had come up and he couldn't make it until the following evening. As I was leaving, I ran into three friends who had seen him. Each was excited by the great changes that had taken place in him. I left without saying much; I felt miserable and disappointed. I walked out into the night, and went home.

I spent most of the night in restless confusion, too agitated for sleep. The whole thing had probably been conjured up in his mind while he was in his weak physical condition. How completely ridiculous to allow myself to become taken in by such a fairy tale.

But somehow the fairy tale kept forcing itself upon me, and I consoled myself with the thought that I would learn much more about the whole matter the next day.

✳ 2 ✳

Extraordinary things like this occur frequently to most of us, but we disregard them, because of our lack of understanding, and think they are mere coincidences.

M Y FRIEND arrived at the club the next evening in a new, high-priced car. We drove in luxury to a nearby restaurant and there, in a private dining room, undisturbed by the presence of others, we had the opportunity to talk.

Some miraculous change had definitely taken place in him. He glowed with health and vitality, and he was calm and poised in a way that inspired admiration and confidence. I felt perfectly at ease in his company, yet I also felt the force of some presence in him that I could neither understand nor describe.

I found it difficult to conceal the emotions I was feeling. I felt convinced he had something I sorely needed, and I had the strangest fear that something might occur that would keep me from getting it.

We were silent at first for a moment, and then he asked if he looked different than he did the day he had left. I had to admit that he was both a revelation and a mystery to me. He began telling his story.

"When I left here, I had made such a mess of my life that I seriously considered suicide, but I feared death too much. I feared life as well, and I couldn't rest. My only relief was to keep moving — I guess I was what you would call a hopeless case.

"In a theater in London, I met a man who is called a Master. I am deeply grateful for the privilege of calling him my friend.

"As I look back on that evening in London, I now realize that my total despair and my intense longing to find something to relieve me drew me and my friend together. I had purchased an inexpensive seat at the theater, but discovered that for some un-explainable reason I had received an expensive box seat instead. Extraordinary things like this occur frequently to most of us, but we disregard them, because of our lack of understanding, and think they are mere coincidences. But I know differently now.

"I could feel that he was aware of my uneasiness, and also that he was an unusual person, for he seemed to have a wonderful kind of radiance about him. I felt an instinctive urge to open my heart to him. Something told me that I had the good fortune of being in the presence of one of those great spiritual people I had read about years ago. Believe it or not, I felt almost immediately at ease just being in his presence.

"After the performance, he invited me to accompany him to a nearby cafe. I noticed that the attention of those in the cafe was drawn to him as we entered, and that the management was especially respectful and courteous toward him. I had the feeling this man possessed some sort of magical power, and I was determined to ask him every question I could think of and — with his permission — take notes of his answers.

"He told me he was taking a cruise ship to New York the next day; I asked if I might accompany him, and he agreed. At the end of our talk, he merely wrote his initials on the bill. As we stepped outside to call a taxi, I asked him if he came to that cafe often. He said it was his first visit to the place, but assured me that the bill would be paid, saying, 'I only initialed it just to show you that with the right attitude you can control every situation.'

"I was puzzled by what he meant, and hoped it would all become clearer to me later.

"That night, as I was half-sleeping in bed, the events of the evening kept passing through my mind. At times I had difficulty believing that my good fortune was real rather than a dream. I was able to sleep peacefully that night, for the first time in months."

* 3 *

Believe me, you can have anything you want — and in abundance — when you learn to tune into the power within, an infinitely greater power than electricity, a power you have had from the beginning.

"*I* GOT UP EARLY the next morning, eager for what the day would bring, and immediately applied for a reservation on the cruise ship. They told me that the passenger list was full, but as I turned away to leave, almost heartbroken, they called to me and said that a reservation had just been cancelled and that I could have it. I felt sure this was more of my friend's 'magic,' as I called it at the time, and I was right, for he later admitted that he had made a place for me.

"At that time I didn't understand how the thing works. But I do now, and it is so simple that its simplicity causes it to be overlooked.

"Anyway, I boarded the cruise ship. My friend arrived with his assistant and, as usual, was surrounded by people eager to help him. I spent most of the voyage with him, and he seemed to enjoy my company.

"The first evening out, I visited him in his stateroom. It was luxuriously furnished — he has the best of everything wherever he goes. He told me about the wonderful forces that we all have, forces we have let lie dormant within us, because of our lack of understanding. He gave several demonstrations of the powers he has developed. He did things that were actually astonishing.

"He asked, 'Why can't you do what I do? Why can't everyone do as I do? I have no powers that you are not endowed with. Here is my answer: Everyone could do as I do, if they had knowledge of Universal Law. I have developed the powers within me, while you have been dissipating and scattering yours, simply because you didn't understand the principles involved. All people use the same power, for in all the universe there is but one power. This rule is self-evident, as you shall see.'

"He continued: 'Most people use the Law destructively, or at least partially so, and the scales are balanced against them. Here and there we occasionally find outstanding people who have achieved success, or greatness. Some of them are considered lucky, some are considered geniuses — but both words are erroneous. Luck and genius actually have very little to do with their success. The fact is they have made use of the Law — whether knowingly or unknowingly, it doesn't matter — sufficiently enough to have the scales balance in their favor. How plain this is to one who knows!'

"He gave me an interesting example: 'Before the discovery of the law governing the use of electricity,' he said, 'this great force was lying dormant throughout the universe, at least as far as humanity was concerned. We first had to discover the law before we could use it to our advantage. It is just the same with this Univeral Law.

" 'Happiness is humanity's rightful heritage; it is the summit of all aspirations. Our souls cry out for happiness, but so many of us misunderstand and think that our ultimate satisfaction can be reached only by making enough *money*. Why is this? Money is but a means to an end. It is the motivation that drives us on in our quest for the ultimate, which is happiness. In this world, it is true, there cannot be fulfillment and happiness without a certain amount of money — the occupation of acquiring money, therefore, is a worthy and commendable one.

" 'Why do so many people suffer all sorts of lack, misery, and unhappiness? It is ridiculous, when you think about it, for people — no matter what their position in life — to believe it is their destiny to lack anything that will contribute to their happiness or that of their families.

" 'Somebody discovers the law governing the use of electricity, and we have radio. Millions of people are now enjoying it. They *tune in* to what they want, and they get it. There is a great lesson in this,

for believe me, you can have anything you want —
and in *abundance* — when you learn to tune in to the
power within, an infinitely greater power than electricity, a power you have had from the beginning.

"'The captain of this ship could just as easily
own it as run it. One position is no more difficult to
attain than another. He tuned in to the captaincy
successfully. Ownership may have *seemed* out of
reach. That's all. The actual difference in the two
positions is merely the difference in two words —
nothing more, as you shall see very clearly when we
get a little further along.'

"Each night I went back to my room and sat up
until early morning, reading my notes and preparing
questions for the next day. He told me that I was very
receptive, because of my eagerness, sincerity, and
trust, and that it was a pleasure to instruct me. I felt
full of gratitude; no price was too high, and no sacrifice was too great, for the knowledge I was receiving.

"I asked him when and how he discovered such
a secret, and he said, 'I discovered nothing, and to me

it is no secret. This knowledge has been in our family as far back as our records go. I use it because I know it to be the easy, certain way of accomplishing a purpose. You have known only the difficult, uncertain way, like most others.'

"He never seemed to want to take credit for anything, always claiming that no credit was due him."

* 4 *

There are no limits to your possibilities! Your successes will multiply and increase in proportion to your mastery of the Law.

"*I*WAS RAPIDLY regaining my health and strength, and was becoming fired with an irresistible ambition to get back and start all over again. I reprimanded myself for having wasted so many valuable years in the fruitless efforts of my old way, and I was eager to start in a new way.

"The voyage passed so quickly! I was soon to part from someone I had become deeply attached to, someone I owed so much. I handed him my card, and asked for his. He said, 'I have no card, no name, no address. I am like the wind. I come from nowhere and I go everywhere. As for my name, just call me Friend.' I said I would rather call him Master, but he said, 'No, no, not Master. Just Friend. That will do.' He glanced at my card and said, 'I turn up at the most unexpected places. I may be out to see you soon. I will write to you.'

"I'll never forget the instructions he gave me as we parted. I felt like a child leaving his parent. He said, 'You are truly fortunate. Just think of the millions of gifted, highly talented people — many blessed with great abilities for success and leadership, whose achievements would mean so much to so many people — who do not know what you know. They go on striving and straining, wasting their precious life force, only to find themselves dissatisfied, discouraged, disheartened, crushed as you once were. Although they are spurred on by that divine spark, that irresistible urge by which they instinctively realize there *is* a way, they cannot find it, and they find themselves failures after years of effort.

"'Now you can avoid all this! Go home; you have learned all that you will need. If you follow the instructions I have given, you can reach any heights. You can accomplish any worthy purpose easily and quickly. There are no limits to your possibilities! Your successes will multiply and increase in proportion to your mastery of the Law. With each success your faith in the Law will grow stronger, until you reach the point of total conviction. Then you will be invincible.

"'Keep in mind the warning I have given you: Reveal nothing of this to even your closest friend. To do so before you are powerfully fortified with the Law will only interfere with your plans; it will result in the scattering of your forces, and weaken their power for your good. So keep your secret locked within your heart. You will never be able to work out someone else's problems, nor will they be able to work out yours. This is strictly a matter for each individual. Accomplishment of anything, in any line, is the result of discovering the operation of this inner force and setting it to work, and this must be done individually. There is no other way.

"'I have no doubt that you will succeed, in every way you wish. The time will come when you will retire from material pursuits, and devote your life to humanity, helping to free it from the bondage of want, misery, and unhappiness.'

"I parted reluctantly from my benefactor. He entered a taxi with his assistant and gave directions to his hotel. I walked down the street, unconscious of the crowds, feeling such a sense of exaltation that I seemed to be floating along rather than walking.

"On the train home, I carefully avoided all unnecessary contact with the other passengers. I kept to myself; I wanted to be alone and think. I couldn't think of sparing any of my precious time for idle conversation — how useless it seemed to me now, when there was so much to be accomplished.

"I was filled with one compelling purpose — to try out my new teaching — and not another day could be wasted. Nothing else interested me and nothing else mattered.

"And that's as much of my story as I can reveal at this time. I hope you find it encouraging, and I hope you will discover more, eventually."

I was disappointed that he couldn't enlighten me further. He assured me he would see that I got in touch with the Master as soon as he arrived. This only intensified my impatience, and I said, "I can't just wait for his arrival — he might never come! Give me the name of his hotel, and I'll go and find him."

He remained calm and poised — which was unusual for him — and replied simply and quietly that he had not overheard the name of the hotel.

* 5 *

I operate according to a definite, unerring law.... I know the outcome before I start.

T HERE WAS NOTHING for me to do but settle down as best as I could and wait and hope, while my friend plunged back into his former occupation in the stock market. He remained quite secretive, and his friends knew little of his affairs, though we met him occasionally at the club. None of us seemed to have the courage to ask him about the changes in his life, and he talked about everything but that. In a short time, however, his activities reached such proportions he had to involve a few of his close friends, including myself. It was then that I learned the magnitude of his endeavors.

I feared that his success could not last, and I attempted to advise him to use greater caution, warning him that some day his bubble would burst. He answered with complete confidence; he said, "You don't have to worry about me. I operate according to a definite, unerring law. If you wanted to get the square footage of this room, you would get the two dimensions, and then, following a process laid down by the law of mathematics, you would get a definite result. You would be certain of the success of the process from the beginning. It's just the same with my work. I know the outcome before I start."

That was the last time I ever questioned his affairs, and he never mentioned them again.

There seemed to be no stopping him. He went from one success to another. His energy and vitality never lagged, and the dynamic force with which he seemed to command every situation and overwhelm all opposition to his progress seemed almost superhuman. At the few social gatherings he attended, his magnetic personality and the mystery his name came to be associated with made him the center of attention.

But he seemed to want to avoid this kind of attention, and I saw very little of him for some time.

I heard no news of the Master, and had just about become resigned to my fate, when my friend's secretary called saying there was a letter at his office that might interest me. It was just a brief note addressed to my friend, written on the stationery of a prominent hotel in a distant city: "Detained by important affairs. Regret to have to cancel a visit to you at this time. Your Friend."

My chance had come at last. The hotel was my only clue, but it was enough. Three interested friends and I quickly left town and drove eastward on our quest for the Master and his secret.

The drive was a long one, but we took turns at the wheel and drove straight through. At the hotel, I went directly to the manager and informed him of our mission. He told me that, because there were so many visitors who were crowding around the Master, he had departed, leaving no address. He had no further information to give us.

Once again I was disheartened. Was I ever to learn his secret? It seemed unlikely. We decided, however, to continue our search. We separated to work more effectively, and continued searching for five days and nights.

On the fifth night, my friends spent an hour trying to persuade me to return home. But I decided that I would not give up. I would continue the search forever, if necessary. They retired to their rooms, and I sat alone in a deserted corner of the lobby until early morning.

Suddenly, my feelings changed from despondency to absolute joy. Somehow, I knew that my search was at an end. I felt a sense of a presence behind me, and then a hand touched my shoulder. I turned and looked into the most magnificent face I have ever seen. His eyes sparkled like jewels!

"Are you looking for me?" he asked.

"I am," I answered, for I knew I had found the man I had been looking for.

We talked briefly. He said he was so busy that there was no way he could give me any instructions, and that he was not even receiving any visitors during his short stay. He promised, however, to contact me as soon as he was available.

I told him that I was desperately in need of him, that we had come thousands of miles to learn his wisdom, and that I was willing to sacrifice anything for just a little of his knowledge. The intensity of my words must have aroused his compassion, for he agreed to receive us for instructions the following morning in his apartment.

* 6 *

If you use these principles wisely and intelligently, there can be no uncertainty as to the outcome of any endeavor, and no limit to your possibilities.

T HE FIRST SIGHT of his apartment will always stand out vividly in my memory. Never before or since have I seen such luxury displayed as in the furnishings of that place. We were led by his assistant through a room delicately perfumed by an abundance of beautifully arranged flowers, across magnificent silk rugs, to a room that appeared to be his study, where chairs had already been placed for us.

He entered immediately, and we had a round of introductions, with names and occupations, and general remarks. I had expected, because of his luxuriant surroundings, to see him extravagantly dressed, but I was struck by the simplicity of both his dress and his bearing. My impression was that, being conscious of his power, he had no need for ostentation and would rather not be the object of any attention. He explained the loveliness of his rooms by simply saying that he loved beautiful things, and therefore surrounded himself with them.

He began our instructions by saying, "You may have come here expecting to see a mysterious being endowed with mystic powers, a sort of magician who can pull a fortune out of the air and pass it over to you. If so, you have very much misled yourselves. I am just an ordinary man, no different than you are. The world calls me a Master. And so I am, but only in the sense that I have learned how to master circumstances and situations in my life. I have developed the powers in me that abide in all of us.

"I realize that you have come here because of your faith in me, and that you hold me in high regard as a successful individual. But in order to gain the greatest benefit from these teachings, I must ask you to wipe out, as fully as you can, any impression you may have of me as a personality. I am worthy of no special honor or special consideration. I am just as human as you are.

I am not superior in any way. I made no discoveries. I received these instructions in much the same way that I am about to give them to you, and I am eternally thankful for the knowledge that I have gained.

"You will have no difficulty in putting these principles into practice in your everyday lives. They are as available to you as to me, for this great Law applies to everyone. It is the highest and most effective Law possible in worldly affairs, and it is well worth learning, for its practice results in a life that is well worth living.

"If you use these principles wisely and intelligently, there can be no uncertainty as to the outcome of any endeavor, and no limit to your possibilities. As you go on, your confidence will increase, and you will find that your powers will increase. You will accomplish greater things with greater ease and greater speed. As its growth in you increases, your accomplishments will increase as well.

"With some people — like your friend who is responsible for your being here today — remarkable improvement comes quickly. With others, the growth is more gradual. The difference is not any difference in the individual, for all of us are endowed with the same capacity, but it is a difference in the degree of intensity employed. No one could ever receive these instructions, however, and not become a better person for them.

"No great things are accomplished in the consciousness of personality; that is impossible, for personality is limiting. You may not understand yet what I mean by this, but you will soon. For now, just remember that it is important to accept these lessons for what they mean to you as an individual. Don't let my presence, or your impression of me, influence you in any way in your studies. Learn from my words only, not from me.

"Now let us proceed."

PART TWO
The Message

∗ 7 ∗

Those who take up any subject with an open mind, willing to learn anything that will contribute to their advancement, comfort, and happiness, are wise.

"AS I GIVE you the principles of this Law, I must ask you to overlook any apparent contradictions, for — of necessity — they are bound to occur when discussing a subject of this kind.

"Keep this advice in mind: Take these teachings for what they mean to you individually. If some of the things I say don't make sense to you or appeal to you at this time, don't force yourself to understand them or accept them. What you may fail to understand or even reject now will no doubt appear plain and become valuable to you later, as your capacity to receive increases.

"There are times when the changing of words makes an idea more clear or more appealing to different people. If you find that replacing my words with your own makes a statement clearer or seems to fit in with your beliefs or mental makeup, you may do so, freely.

"Those who think they know everything will learn nothing. Those who approach a subject with doubt and resistance will learn very little. There is not much hope for them. But those who take up any subject with an open mind, willing to learn anything that will contribute to their advancement, comfort, and happiness, are wise.

"Although I don't ask that you believe all that I tell you — for to do so would be to interfere with your freedom of thought — I ask you to try not to doubt or resist what I tell you, for that will prevent you from gaining the help you are seeking. For your own highest and greatest good, your attitude should be just this: 'I am going to listen to these teachings with an open-minded, neutral attitude, determined to gain all the benefits they offer me. The fact that I don't understand or even believe a particular statement or proposition at this time doesn't necessarily make it any less true.'

"To make use of the Law, it's necessary that you have a clear understanding of its operation. To help you gain this understanding, I will illustrate, whenever possible, with examples that you will find all around you and that will help you understand these truths.

"Your mind can be likened to a house that has been cluttered over the years with thousands of unnecessary pieces of furniture, pictures, ornaments, and other things, all strewn around and piled everywhere. The result is that, although the outside of the house may present a good appearance, the inside is a mess of confusion and disorder. It is impossible to accomplish anything under such conditions, for you cannot go after one thing without stumbling over another. There is no order. No purpose. No progress. The first necessary thing to do, then, is to rid that house of all but the furnishings that are essential to your success."

✳ 8 ✳

Any picture firmly held in any mind, in any form, is bound to come forth. That is the great, unchanging Universal Law that, when we cooperate with it intelligently, makes us absolute masters of the conditions and situations in our lives.

"CONSIDER THIS: How did you get here? You grew from a minute cell much smaller than the point of a pin. Just think! A cell or seed the size of a pinpoint contained within itself in essence and in entirety the complex, wonderful being that you are today.

"Surely, that cell could not possibly contain the physical forms, no matter how infinitesimal they may be, of your body, head, hair, arms, legs, hands, feet, and all the wonderful organs of your body. Well, then, how did you arrive at your full stature as you are today? That cell contained within it a spark of

Mind; that cell had the power, true to the law of its own being, to hold a *fixed image* or picture of you, and you unfolded, grew, and eventually 'out-pictured,' or became objectified in obedience to that law.

"If this wording doesn't appeal to you, your reasoning will certainly admit that there is a power at work in that cell that unfolds according to a definite plan. So, an intelligence of some form has to be present. The presence of this intelligence is what I mean when I say that cell contains a spark of Mind.

"It is necessary at this point to get one fact clear, for it is the fundamental basis from which we proceed, and that point is this: Mind, no matter what form it is apparently contained in, holds images, pictures. And *any picture firmly held in any mind, in any form, is bound to come forth.* That is the great, unchanging Universal Law that, when we cooperate with it intelligently, makes us absolute masters of the conditions and situations in our lives.

"Can you recall instances when you secretly had a desire within yourself for some particular thing — and within a short time, it became yours? Or times when you felt you might meet a particular person — and, shortly after, that person appeared? You may have said, 'What a coincidence! I was thinking of you just this morning!' But it's no coincidence at all. It's not at all strange. It was the natural outcome of the operation of a definite law.

"If this is true, why don't *all* our wishes or thoughts appear? Many of them do, but because of our lack of awareness, because of our ignorance of Universal Law, they pass unnoticed. Then again, many don't manifest at all. I can use your knowledge of radio to illustrate why. Have you ever wanted to tune into one particular station when there were one or more other stations competing for the same spot on the dial? The result is a jumble of confusion. But if you reach that station when the others are temporarily off, you get it clearly, and your desire is gratified.

"In just the same way, if our thoughts or desires arise at just the instant when there are no conflicting thoughts present to nullify their power, the mind, instead of being divided among many thoughts, throws its great force behind that one desire. That desire becomes 'out-pictured,' or externalized.

"You have all experienced times when your mind became a complete blank for just a moment, and you found yourself staring into space. If at that instant it were possible to inject any wish, any desire, with sufficient force, nothing on earth could prevent it from coming forth, very quickly.

"Now, what is the cause of the confusion prevailing in your mind that weakens your thought? It is the false belief that there is a power or powers outside you greater than the power within you.

"But if through a system of practice, conditions within you became such that every constructive thought was automatically externalized, you would be master of all conditions or circumstances that affect your lives.

"There is but one way to prove whether this is true or not — and that is to try it!"

* 9 *

Words are feeble things when one attempts to explain these deeper things of Universal Law. You have to gradually and patiently advance up to them and into them to really understand.

"THE NEXT STEP in your instructions is this: *The consciousness or fixed picture in mind of anything, any condition, any circumstance is the actual thing itself.* What you experience through the five senses is the mental image out-pictured or made visible or tangible, the same as the artist who puts mental pictures upon a canvas. The artist's hand is merely the instrument the mind expresses through; the artist's hand is under the guidance and direction of the mind.

"Scientists tell us that all of the cells in your entire body die and are passed off at such a rate that you do not possess one cell of the body you had a year ago. But you remember many years back, don't you? You can recall many childhood memories. How can you remember back through those many years, when all of your brain cells have renewed themselves? Because you are *Mind*. You are *not* body.

"As an individual entity, functioning in an individual sphere — which is true of each of us — *you* are all-powerful Mind, and your body is the vehicle through which you function. You are master and your body is your servant. It is your instrument of expression. That is all.

"Now, which is the real body — the one that remains pictured or imaged forever in mind as long as you exist here, or the one that decays in its entirety and passes into the earth every year? And which are the real things — those things imaged or pictured in mind, or those things seen in the outer world that disintegrate after a short existence?

"I don't wish to mislead you with the impression that the outer world is of little or no importance in human achievement, but it is only secondary. A fundamental knowledge of the operation of mind is of primary importance to you at the start.

"I wish it were possible to clearly explain, so that you could easily understand, the process by which a picture in mind becomes objectified, but it would require hours even to make an effort in this direction, and then I might only confuse you. For words are feeble things when one attempts to explain these deeper things of Universal Law. You must gradually and patiently advance up to them and into them to really understand. Fortunately, it is not necessary to know this to use the Law any more than it is necessary to know the law by which the sun's rays are transmitted to earth to enjoy them. You have faith in my sincerity of purpose. Very well, put the same amount of faith in the power of this Law, and anything you undertake will be possible to accomplish.

"Now, let's get on to the next step."

✷ 10 ✷

As electricity is a great power in the world, so the Inner Mind is the greatest power available to you. Neither operates independently; both depend upon a separate agency to incite them to action, and both bring helpful or harmful results according to the wisdom or ignorance with which they are directed.

"YOU MAY HAVE HEARD it said that there are many minds, but such a statement is merely an idiom, a common expression. There is nothing in science or reality to support such a statement. There is but one mind, as there is but one electricity or one atmosphere. The many minds referred to are but a multiplicity of expressions of the one. We use mind as we use air or electricity — as our individual needs require.

"Now I have to ask you to bear with me for a time while I make use of a contradiction so that I may

47

explain the next subject. At this point, I have to mention *three* minds — or, properly speaking, three phases of mind.

"You are apparently made up of three minds. The one that controls the functioning of the body, for want of a better word, I will call the Deeper Mind. This mind we are not particularly concerned with and properly should not be. It knows its functions better than we do. We can cooperate with this mind, and benefit greatly in our health and strength, by keeping our thoughts off the body. By not interfering with the proper functioning of the Deeper Mind, we find that it gets along very nicely.

"It is the other two minds that we are deeply interested in: what I call the Inner and Outer Minds.

"The appropriate function of the Outer Mind, which is in touch with external things through the medium of the five senses, is to transmit its desires to the Inner Mind, which is the seat of power within you and which, by its very nature, has no consciousness of duality because it has no faculty of discrimination. It knows no impossibility, no failure, no obstacle, no limit to anything or lack of anything. It depends upon the guidance of the Outer Mind and throws its great, unlimited force into anything that the Outer Mind may direct it toward.

"I can explain the nature of the Inner Mind by comparing it again with electricity. As electricity is a great power in the world, so the Inner Mind is the greatest power available to you. Neither operates independently; both depend upon a separate agency to incite them to action, and both bring helpful or harmful results according to the wisdom or ignorance with which they are directed.

"You can see how important it is, then, for the Outer Mind to unite with the Inner, and cooperate with it! If this were the case in human activities, people would be masters of their circumstances, instead of slaves.

"Why aren't we all masters of our circumstances in life? For this reason: The Outer Mind forms a desire; this desire is automatically taken up by the Inner Mind, which immediately sets to work bringing it forth. But the Inner Mind scarcely has time to turn its great force in that direction before the Outer has either found a new desire, or has conjured up illusionary obstacles to the desire. The Inner Mind, not being on the surface, not in contact with outer things, and consequently dependent upon the Outer Mind for guidance, is forced to divert its power. And so it goes, on and on, like leaks in a steam pipe, scattering its wonderful power everywhere but getting nowhere.

"Why is the Inner Mind thwarted in this way every time it moves toward accomplishment? Because the Outer Mind judges everything by what the eye and ear report, and transmits those messages to the Inner Mind.

"What do we find people doing? We find them *taking pictures* of what they experience daily in the outer world, then *printing* those pictures upon themselves within. The procedure should be *just the reverse*.

"We have the capacity and the power to create desirable pictures within, and to find them automatically printed in the outer world of our surroundings. And it is a simple process, as you will see later. When we can do this, we have mastery. And not before.

"Well, then, you would think that what we need to do is to discipline the Outer Mind, because it seems to be the offender. And that's right. But because it encounters thousands of experiences every day, ordinary methods of training may require years to accomplish results. Or, at best, such training would be a long, drawn-out process. There is a quicker and better way, a method that makes skillful use of the Outer Mind. And the first step in this method follows."

✴ *11* ✴

If we are to accomplish anything in a big way, a set definite objective must be established.

"SUPPOSE THERE IS an urgent need for you to reach a certain town as quickly as possible. When you step into your automobile, you naturally *picture in mind* your destination, and you head in that direction. If you're uncertain of the way, you might take a wrong turn and head in the wrong direction, but eventually you find the way to get to your destination. You are guided by the *picture in mind* of the place you are headed for, and you get there.

"You held to a *set definite objective* until you reached it. You held your objective or destination in mind without any particular effort or strain, and you returned to the proper route when you found you had strayed. It is the same with us: *A set definite objective* must be established if we are to accomplish anything in a big way.

"What do I mean by establishing a set definite objective? Is it as simple as it sounds? No, at least not at the start. Would you set your objective at making a million dollars immediately, overnight? Yes, you might, if you have the capacity to see a million dollars as an immediate possibility. But that's quite rare. The wise thing to do is to grow to it as marathon runners do, by first running a mile, then two miles, then three, gradually expanding their capacity to eventually cover the full distance.

"Why is a set definite objective necessary? There are three reasons. First, the Inner Mind is the positive pole of your being, and the Outer is the negative pole. There must be a positive and negative in everything in the universe to complete a circuit or a circle, or there would be no activity, no motion. There would be no forward if we had no backward. There could be no up if there were no down. There could never be such a thing as good if there were no so-called evil. How could there be light without darkness? For us to be conscious of one thing, there must be an opposite to compare it with, or else it remains nonexistent for us.

"Now, in everything that is obedient to the Law, the positive dominates and governs, and the negative serves. But humanity reverses this: The Outer Mind looks upon the world and reports strife, competition, obstacles, impossibilities, and similar conditions. Why? Because of the absence of direction, it is left to wander without a purpose — and aimlessly wandering, it accepts everything.

"The set definite objective firmly imaged or pictured in mind immediately whips the Outer into line by giving it a *fixed duty* to perform. This, automatically, without any effort on your part, infuses it with the positive quality of the Inner Mind. And again, automatically, positive conditions and individuals are attracted to you as surely as steel particles are attracted to a magnet. That's the first reason why a set definite objective is necessary.

"Second, the atmosphere is filled with millions upon millions of thoughts, forever in motion. The hundreds of radio stations in this country, all broadcasting simultaneously, give you a slight idea of the thoughts in the air. Every human being is a broadcasting station and everybody is a receiving set. This explains why I am able to answer your questions instantly, before you have had to form them into words. The fact is, I have been receiving your thoughts before you have expressed them. This is a faculty developed after years of training. This faculty was always in me and is in you as well. I have brought out and made use of mine; yours lies almost entirely dormant.

"People who have no set definite objectives are tuning in to everything and getting nothing. They are unfortunate indeed, for they are at the mercy of millions of conflicting thoughts, and their lives are full of confusion and distress.

"People who have definite objectives, on the other hand, deliberately tune in to *one thing*. If it is money, they get it. If it is position, they get it. Nothing that such people tune in to can be withheld.

"Third, when you set your mind on anything, whether it be small or large, tangible or intangible — a pencil, a hat, an automobile, a home, great riches, an education, a profession, or travel — you transfer a portion of your life force to that thing, otherwise it could not be drawn to you. And you continue to nourish it as long as you hold it in mind, and the intensity of your desire governs the power with which the force is directed.

"So you can see that if you direct that force at several objectives, it becomes divided, and each objective receives a fairly weak stimulus, which results in a slow reaction, or no reaction at all. Do you have a great, ultimate goal to reach that requires attaining lesser objectives along the way? Well then, let the many lie inactive and direct your force at the nearest or first; once you accomplish that, take up the next, and so on.

"Now, have I given you the Law in its entirety? In a sense I have. Then again, I have not. To instruct you as to what to do is good, but to show you how to do it is better. It is not only necessary that we learn how to attain, but we must also learn how to maintain. So I will go further, and give you an important requirement in successful achievement: that is *secretiveness*."

✳ *12* ✳

When you work in the Inner Mind, you invoke and receive the help of the impersonal, unlimited resources of the universe.

"BEFORE I EXPLAIN the value of secretiveness, I have to start with another subject.

"When you declare 'I am,' 'I will,' 'I did,' you are making a profound and mighty statement. There are very few who realize the power released when the 'I' is expressed. Hear the great proclamation, 'I AM THAT I AM,' which has lived and resounded through the ages and which, when understood, unites each one of us with that impersonal, universal power.

"The body you have is personal, but the 'I' you express is universal, for in all the universe there is but one 'I,' as in all the universe there is but one number *one*. The other numbers are but multiples or derivatives of that *one*. The number *seven*, for instance, is *one* repeated so many times. It is the understanding of those in my work that the 'I' is the root from which the number *one* has sprung.

"From what I have said, you should be able to see this: When you work in the Outer Mind, you are working from a personal, limited standpoint. When you work in the Inner Mind, you invoke and receive the help of the impersonal, unlimited resources of the universe. Well, you ask, how am I to arrive at this state? Easily, I say: by merely following the system of practice I am outlining, you naturally gravitate into it unknowingly.

"Since the great and mighty 'I' is, when expressed individually, none other than yourself, you can see what power you have at your command. You can see what a wonderful being you are. You can see that you are *now* a master, not yet developed perhaps, but the qualities are there waiting to unfold and be of use.

"If you don't clearly understand what I have just said, let it pass for now and we'll go on to the next idea. You can later reason it out for yourself and see the truth of it.

"You might question the value of such a detailed explanation, but I have a purpose, and that purpose is to force you to think, to think deeply, with intensity. Don't confuse the word 'intensity' with 'tenseness.' Tenseness implies mental strain, and arises out of fear and anxiety. It is destructive to both mind and body. My use of intensity here suggests mental force or power, and its results are constructive.

"Your progress depends upon your degree of sustained intensity in a given direction. You know that progress is becoming very rapid these days. We must travel as rapidly as the world or give up, and when we give up we immediately begin to backslide. To enjoy enduring success, we should travel a little in advance of the world.

"The persistent inner urge in humanity to reach an objective more speedily eventually crystallized and out-pictured itself in the form of an automobile, which was the first big step in fast transportation for general use. But since it is the nature of Mind to forever reach out for greater achievement, the airplane came into being. And thus Mind moves and thus it will move forever.

"Open your eyes and look around you and you can certainly see the trend. Mind is forever reaching out, and has not stopped at the airplane as a rapid mode of travel. The person who knows the Law and uses it is supreme; those that are ignorant, who refuse to see this, just remain in bondage to their false beliefs. It is so important, then, to learn to *think things through* rather than follow the time-worn method of attempting to *force* them through. One is mastery and the other slavery.

"The value of secretiveness lies in the fact that, being impersonal and universal, the 'I' throws its power in with whatever words it is coupled, and when your plans are expressed verbally, they become released and their force is spent. The Outer Mind has found a way of escape, and your purpose has lost its necessary momentum."

✳ *13* ✳

*It is your rightful heritage, your birthright, to have any-
thing that you desire, without limit.*

"THE NEXT REQUIREMENT is something I call
your *nourishment*, or *reserve*. Very few people are
really capable of sustained effort, and that's the reason
why we have comparatively few outstanding successes.

"You have learned that your great power lies not
on the surface, but deep within your being, in your
Inner Mind. Average people live on the surface, un-
aware of their great inner power. They place what little faith they have in the Outer Mind, and they are
governed by its false reports. As a result, they are
constantly in a turmoil of confusion, strife, and strain
until they succumb, discouraged and disheartened,
broken in health and spirit.

"Why is this so? Why is it such a common belief
that people who accumulate wealth have to pay

dearly for it with their health and vitality? Because, as I have told you, when they focus their efforts upon a given objective, they automatically transfer a portion of their vital life force to it. This is all very well and necessary, but if they continue this practice without replenishing that life force, without nourishing themselves, they become drained, and the results are always some kind of trouble.

"It is your rightful heritage, your birthright, to have anything that you desire, without limit. Those things that you desire were put here for you to use and enjoy. If not, why are they here? And since only *you* can be conscious of *your* own individual desires, those things were placed here specifically for you.

"Yes, you *can* have riches and position, and health and happiness as well, when you *know* the law of your being and cooperate with it. I have no patience with those who say that poverty is a blessing. Poverty is the greatest curse on earth. Those who preach such a doctrine are untrue to themselves, for, at the same time they are preaching the blessings of poverty, the desire for the good things of life is gnawing at their hearts.

"Each individual that is given the fundamental principles of the Law will work it out somewhat differently, according to his or her own particular inherent nature. I have purposely avoided referring to *my* method, so that you might have your own freedom of interpretation, and freedom to make your own decisions. But I want to give you a hint of how I work, though I have to advise you not to let this influence or change you in *your* particular method. You cannot attain mastery by patterning yourself after another, or by following custom or tradition. Sheep and plodders do that. Masters and leaders never do.

"A painting would be a dull, uninteresting thing if the artist, in featuring a great oak tree, failed to include its natural surroundings of grass, brush, flowers, leaves, and possibly sky and clouds. The artist creates a faithful reproduction of nature. Our methods are similar: While he places his picture upon a canvas, I place mine within. He places the oak upon a canvas and gives it its natural surroundings. I do the same. To bring his picture forth, he concentrates upon it to the exclusion of all else that would tend to draw him away from his purpose. So do I. At times something in the external world suggests the picture to him; at other times inspiration suggests it. It is the same with me. A hundred things in a day may come up to distract him and attempt to draw him away, but his picture is of paramount importance. He does not resist those distractions, but gives them their due attention and returns to the picture. Just so with me. When his picture is completed, he begins another. I do too. For I am never consciously, mentally inactive. Inactivity is retrogression.

"Here's a concrete example: If I desire the presence of my assistant at this moment, I see him before me in the picture of my mind, surrounded by what is within my vision here. Soon after, the image 'outpictures.'

"Were I to desire wealth, I would surround that picture with everything I instinctively feel would accompany that wealth, all the conditions and possessions that I would naturally want to include. If necessary, I would get my suggestions from the out-picturing or externalized picture of another's success. I would go about my duties as usual. It matters little what I appear to be doing in the outer world. It matters a great deal what I am doing within.

"If I were a beginner and desired, for instance, a new automobile or home, I would select a picture closely resembling the one I desired from a magazine, and place it where I would see it frequently. This holds the Outer Mind in line and hastens the out-picturing of my idea."

✳ 14 ✳

These powerful words automatically help you to discover and meet your needs. They act upon your Outer and Inner Mind very much like the nutrients in your food act upon your body.

"NOW YOU ARE READY for a simple but very effective exercise: I will give you a list of powerful words that not only tend to keep the life force nourished, but will give you all the strength you need for doing the internal work necessary to create what you want in life. Here is my list — you can certainly add to it if you wish:

Concentration	Charity
Peace	Nonresistance
Poise	Justice
Harmony	Consideration
Goodwill	Freedom
Honesty	Guidance

Wisdom	Activity
Kindness	Generosity
Understanding	Vitality
Inspiration	Compassion
Humility	Power
Intelligence	Serenity
Decision	Love
Memory	Tolerance
Sympathy	Gentleness
Law	Creativity
Grace	Life
Faith	Youth
Confidence	Courtesy
Abundance	Success
Merit	Happiness
Spirit	Alertness
Health	Resourcefulness
Unity	Persistence
Strength	Purpose
Sincerity	Achievement
Energy	Mastery
Capability	

"After a day's activity, when your ordinary duties and affairs have depleted your life force a bit, it is a good idea to set aside half an hour — or an hour, if possible — each evening when you can be alone and undisturbed, in the quiet and stillness of your own being. Select words from the list that seem appropriate to your needs at the moment, or simply begin with the first word and move down the list at your own pace. *Firmly impress* your being with each word, at the same time interpreting its meaning and noticing its effect upon you, not necessarily in the terms of its generally accepted meaning, but strictly as it appeals to you.

"I repeatedly stress the fact that you are the 'I,' the power in *your* world, and that you are to stand on your own two feet firmly and *live it* — not necessarily display it, but live it. I don't advise, however, that you use the declaration 'I am' in connection with the words in this list unless you are in a positive frame of mind at the time, unless you have full conviction of what you are repeating.

"For example, if you declare 'I am Power,' you lay the Inner Mind open to attack from the Outer in

71

the form of denial or doubt. But if you repeat only the words on the list — such as simply saying *'Power'* to yourself — the words do not have the nature of a declaration, and the Outer Mind is not as likely to deny or doubt.

"To get into the right attitude during this practice, try to at least momentarily keep your thoughts off your body and off external affairs and things; this automatically places you in the ideal mood. Of course, the Outer Mind will wander and bring up hundreds of things, hundreds of times, but like the automobile that I mentioned straying off course, bring it back and back again, each time setting it on the right road. This tendency of the Outer Mind to wander will gradually decrease during these periods, and you will soon find yourself becoming a master of concentration.

"There should be no strain, striving, anxiety, or concern connected with this practice. Devote each evening to it, unless otherwise taken up by occasional business, social, or family duties. Allow these words to sink in and penetrate your being, and like drops of pure water entering a vessel of impure water, the non-essentials are forced out, drop by drop, and eventually the essentials remain.

"These powerful words automatically help you to discover and meet your needs. They act upon your Outer and Inner Mind very much like the nutrients in your food act upon your body. Don't look for results from this practice, any more than you look for results from what you eat every day. Practice this meditation every evening, as regularly as you can, and then forget about the exercise, until the next evening. The words will be doing their work below the surface unknown to you, and their effects will soon show forth in you and in your affairs."

*Whoever or whatever it is you resist — whether in
thought, word, or action, in the form of criticism, envy,
jealousy, hatred, or otherwise — you most assuredly help,
and you weaken yourself proportionately.*

"WHEN YOU INVOKE the aid of this Law, you do not need money, friends, or influence to attain whatever your heart is set upon.

"It doesn't matter in the least what your position is in life. It doesn't matter whether your ambition is directly in line with the position you now occupy, or whether it requires a complete change from what you are doing. You may have no definite plan in life except the fact that you want to get ahead. All the desire in the world will get you nowhere; what is necessary to do first is to establish a *set definite objective* firmly within.

"So, after much thought, you decide on one supreme goal. Even if it is distant, be assured that *it can be attained.* What is your first step? If you have your own business, is it a definite increase in monthly volume? Or, if you are an employee, is it a promotion with a raise in pay? Define your first and nearest goal in the direction of your supreme objective.

"When the first objective is reached, what then? Set another one beyond that, *immediately.* Why? Because the peculiar nature of the Outer Mind is to drop back into inertia after achieving an objective. You can imagine the Outer Mind saying something like this: 'Well, I have been mercilessly driven, and forced to attain that goal, and now that I've reached it I'm going to rest.' And your answer will be, 'No rest for you, for I've already started you on another.' Once you have attained that valuable momentum, *maintain it.* Cling to it. And as the momentum increases, the steps in your progress become more rapid, until eventually it's possible to reach an objective almost immediately.

"The course you follow in creating your objective is exactly like the process that takes place in a seed. Once the seed is planted in the darkness of the soil, it proceeds to express or out-picture the exact picture held within its life cell and, in obedience to law, it sends up a shoot seeking the light. At the same time, it sends down roots seeking nourishment. If, on the way up, that shoot encounters obstacles in any form, it does not attempt to force them out of its way. It travels around them. If the roots fail to find the required nourishment, it withers away. If all goes well, it blossoms forth and, having reached its goal, a seed is again dropped and the process is repeated. Keep in mind that the actual process takes place in darkness, beneath the surface. It is the same with us. That is where all great and important ideas are developed.

"Now, are you going to constantly be glancing out of the corner of your eye to see how things are proceeding? Are you going to be wondering how the thing works, or if it really is working? Not at all. You set the objective. You planted the seed. You wouldn't dig up a seed in your garden to see if it were sprouting. You planted and watered it, and you're satisfied that, according to the law of its being, it will come forth. In exactly the same way, nothing on earth can prevent your objective from becoming externalized, because nothing in the world can nullify Universal Law. You plant the seed idea. You hold it there. You nourish it. You have done your part. Trust the Law to do its part.

"Will you encounter resistance? Oh, yes! Your activity creates it. Why? Because action requires reaction to support it. Resistance is the negative pole, and action or activity is the positive pole, and you need both. If there were no resistance, action would be impossible.

"It is resistance that keeps an airplane in the air. Without resistance, it couldn't fly. Birds couldn't fly either; fish couldn't swim; you couldn't walk. As the power of the engine increases, the greater the momentum of the airplane and the greater the resistance necessary to support it. The greater the momentum, the greater the altitude that is possible to attain.

"This is a good example for us. Momentum must be attained and then *maintained* if we are to reach the heights of achievement. And after the apparent difficulty of the first steps are passed, the work is delightful. For there is nothing more joyous than the satisfaction of having achieved something worthwhile.

"Remember this great truth: Whoever or whatever it is you resist — whether in thought, word, or action, in the form of resentment, criticism, envy, jealousy, hatred, or otherwise — you most assuredly *help*, and you *weaken* yourself proportionately. Why? Because you have deliberately taken a portion of your precious life force so necessary to your progress, and transferred it to that person or thing. Have you ever witnessed someone becoming exhausted after a fit of rage? Exhaustion is depletion. Something went out, to the other person's benefit and to your loss. This is an example of the transfer of life force, in a violent form.

"You are very fortunate to have learned this wisdom. Now, by all means, *practice it.*"

* *16* *

Take the position that you are master of your being, and hold your course firmly to your goal.

"AS YOU PRACTICE these teachings, what should your attitude be? What is the attitude of the wind as it speeds on its way to its destination? It recognizes no person, place, or thing as having any power to hinder it. It is *impersonal*. The sun shines, the rain falls, and the wind blows upon all alike. They choose no particular persons or things to help or harm.

"There is a lesson in that. Those who attempt to hinder you are *helping* you, and they should be considered your friends. This is wisdom of the highest order.

"Keep the secret of your aspirations locked securely within you. This sets up antagonism in the Outer Mind, for it rebels against discipline and control.

"Seeing that it is about to be deprived of its freedom, it will, like a wild bull in a stockade, seek to escape by every means except the way you have provided. I am warning you — it will bring every sort of argument it can in an attempt to convince you that your purpose is futile. It will tempt you to mention your plans and ambitions to others, to slow up your activity, to doubt the power of the Law operating in your behalf. It will try in every conceivable way to thwart you. And your answer to all this will be, '*Obey. I am master here.*' Take the position that you are master of your being, and hold your course firmly to your goal.

"You may be led through strange places and take circuitous routes at times, but don't let that disturb you. With the wisdom of the Inner Mind at the helm, you are being led the quickest way, even though it may appear at times to be the longest.

"This advice is necessary for you now as beginners, but as you grow in practice you will find that these qualities become a part of your very being. Then they function automatically, without any conscious effort at all on your part.

"What is the result? When you persistently hold to your goal, and keep absolutely air-tight secretiveness, the Outer Mind finds no escape for its increasing energy, and in desperation it plunges through, like the overload of steam through the safety valve of a boiler, and your objective is reached.

"We have come to the close of your instructions. Now it is up to you to go out and practice what you know. Living the Law will cause you to become the kind of individual that people notice. They will be instinctively attracted to you, without knowing why, on the street and in your social and business affairs. You will become a mysterious being to the world. Don't let this go to your head. Give thanks, in humble gratitude, to the great Supreme Power that has made this possible."

New World Library is dedicated to publishing books and cassettes that help improve the quality of our lives. If you enjoyed *The Message of a Master*, we highly recommend the following books from New World Library:

As You Think by James Allen. An updated and revised edition of *As a Man Thinketh*, this classic has inspired readers for nearly a century. (Also available on cassette.)

The Instant Millionaire by Mark Fisher. An original fable loaded with specific financial advice. (Also available on cassette.)

Creative Visualization by Shakti Gawain. This international bestseller with over two million copies in print, gives us easy and effective ways to use our imagination to create the life we want.

The Perfect Life by Marc Allen. This powerful book shows you step by step how to map a course that moves you toward the realization of your dreams.

For a complete catalog of our fine books and cassettes, contact:

New World Library
58 Paul Drive, San Rafael, CA 94903
Phone: (415) 472-2100
FAX: (415) 472-6131

Or call toll free:

(800) 227-3900; in California (800) 632-2122